Eli Manning
A Football Star
Who Cares

Barry Wilner

Enslow Elementary
an imprint of
Enslow Publishers, Inc.

40 Industrial Road
Box 398
Berkeley Heights, NJ 07922
USA

http://www.enslow.com

Enslow Elementary, an imprint of Enslow Publishers, Inc.
Enslow Elementary® is a registered trademark of Enslow Publishers, Inc.

Library of Congress Cataloging-in-Publication Data

Wilner, Barry.
  Eli Manning : a football star who cares / Barry Wilner.
     p. cm. — (Sports stars who care)
  Includes bibliographical references and index.
  Summary: "Follow Eli Manning's journey from childhood to becoming a Pro Bowl and Super Bowl winning
quarterback. This sports biography shows how Eli is an all-star on and off the field, and really is a sports star who
cares"—Provided by publisher.
  ISBN 978-0-7660-4300-8
  1. Manning, Eli, 1981—Juvenile literature. 2. Football players—United States—Biography—Juvenile
literature. I. Title.
  GV939.M2887W55 2013
  796.332092—dc23
  [B]
                          2012039419

Future editions:
Paperback ISBN: 978-1-4644-0545-7   EPUB ISBN: 978-1-4645-1278-0
Single-User PDF ISBN: 978-1-4646-1278-7   Multi-User PDF ISBN: 978-0-7660-5910-8

Printed in the United States of America

052013 Lake Book Manufacturing, Inc., Melrose Park, IL

10 9 8 7 6 5 4 3 2 1

To Our Readers: We have done our best to make sure all Internet addresses in this book were active and appropri-
ate when we went to press. However, the author and the Publisher have no control over, and assume no liability for,
the material available on those Internet sites or on other Web sites they may link to. Any comments or suggestions
can be sent by e-mail to comments@enslow.com or to the address on the back cover.

♻ Enslow Publishers, Inc., is committed to printing our books on recycled paper. The paper in every book contains 10% to 30% post-consumer waste (PCW). The cover board on the outside of each book contains 100% PCW.
Our goal is to do our part to help young people and the environment too!

Photo Credits: AP Images/Bebeto Matthews, p. 41; AP Images/Bill Kostroun, pp. 32, 35; AP Images/Darron
Cummings, p. 6; AP Images/David Drapkin, pp. 1, 9, 17, 29; AP Images/David J. Phillip, p. 11; AP Images/David
Rae Morris, p. 20; AP Images/David Stluka, p. 38; AP Images/Donna McWilliam, p. 27; AP Images for Sears/
Gregory Smith, p. 42; AP Images/Jack Thornell, p. 19; AP Images/Julie Jacobson, p. 30; AP Images/Ric Tapia, p.
4; AP Images/Rogelio Solis, pp. 23, 25; AP Images/Stephen Savoia, p. 37; AP Images/Tom Hauck, p. 14.

Cover Photo: AP Images/David Drapkin

Contents

It is not easy being the youngest brother, especially when your older siblings are football stars.

Add in the father being a College Football Hall of Fame player who spent 14 seasons in the NFL.

For Eli Manning, it wound up being a great way to grow up.

Eli is seven years younger than his oldest brother, Cooper, and five years younger than Peyton, the middle son of Archie and Olivia Manning. Archie was an All-America quarterback at the University of Mississippi, and he taught his sons well.

Cooper, a wide receiver, played one season at Ole Miss before a back injury ended his career. Peyton became one of college football's greatest quarterbacks. Then he moved to the NFL with the Indianapolis Colts, playing every game from his rookie year of 1998. He won four league MVP awards until a neck injury forced him to miss the 2011 season. Peyton returned in 2012 to win the Comeback Player of the Year award.

Like Archie, Eli went to the University of Mississippi and had a brilliant career. Eli won several national awards and led the Rebels to two bowl victories. And like Peyton, Eli was the first overall selection in the NFL draft.

But unlike Peyton, who was eager to get going in Indianapolis, Eli and his dad preferred he not be

From left to right, Archie, Peyton, Cooper, and Eli Manning.

picked by San Diego at the top of the 2004 draft. They asked the Chargers to choose someone else. But Eli was taken with the first pick anyway and even posed for photos with a San Diego cap on.

A few minutes later, he was wearing a different hat: The New York Giants traded Philip Rivers, another standout college quarterback whom they had selected, and a bunch of draft picks, to get Manning.

Eli was headed to New York.

And the Giants were headed for big things.

How big?

Try two Super Bowl championships, both in upset wins over New England. In the 2008 title game, Eli lifted the Giants past an unbeaten Patriots team with a dramatic fourth-quarter comeback. Four years later, he did the same thing, giving Eli one more Super Bowl ring than Peyton owned.

Eli had become so popular that he even hosted *Saturday Night Live* on television, something Peyton did a few years before. The little brother had grown into a superstar.

As the New York Giants walked off the field following their final game of the 2007 schedule, they were spirited and confident. Yes, they had just lost 38–35 to New England, the 16th win in the Patriots' perfect regular season. But they also had given the Patriots a very tough test, which they knew could help them as they entered the NFL playoffs as a wild-card team.

Chapter 1

Beating the Unbeatable

Eli Manning calls an audible to change the play during the last game of the 2007 regular season.

"We didn't win the game, but if you saw everybody in the locker room, everybody was excited," Eli Manning said after one of his best performances. He had completed 22 of 32 passes for 251 yards and four touchdowns. "I never saw a locker room so upbeat after a loss because we played so well, did some good things, and hung in there in a game where we didn't have to play. We wanted to. We wanted to come out and play well, and we did that."

Still, the Giants needed to play terrific football to get another chance at the Patriots, which could only happen in the Super Bowl. Manning would do his best to get them there, even though every game would be on the road.

But the Giants were comfortable away from home, going 7–1 during the season. And in their first postseason trip, to Tampa, their defense controlled the game in a 24–14 win. It was Manning's first playoff victory.

Then the Giants went to Dallas, which had beaten them in both regular-season matchups. The Cowboys had won the NFC East with a 13–3 record to New

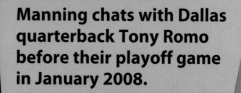

Manning chats with Dallas quarterback Tony Romo before their playoff game in January 2008.

York's 10–6. The Cowboys scored 76 points in those two wins against the Giants.

This time Dallas got only 17, while Manning threw for two touchdowns in a 21–17 victory. Suddenly, Eli and the Giants were in the NFC Championship Game against Green Bay. Oddly, older brother Peyton, who led Indianapolis to the NFL title the year before, was knocked out of the playoffs a few hours earlier.

"I was a little nervous," Eli admitted. "I know (Peyton) was watching and rooting for me."

Peyton next would root for little brother against the Packers at famous Lambeau Field. Few visiting teams win there, particularly in the playoffs. Eli, who spent most of his life before entering the NFL living in warmer weather in the South, would have to prove himself in freezing temperatures, too. The forecast called for a temperature of minus-3 degrees F with a windchill of minus-24.

Yet, Manning was on fire. Shrugging off the numbing chill, he brought the Giants back late in the game. Then in overtime, Lawrence Tynes's field goal won the third-coldest championship match ever.

"We knew we could compete with anybody," Manning said. "It's just a matter of getting hot at the right time."

An even hotter team awaited, though: New England. Again.

The Patriots set all kinds of records on offense during their perfect regular season. They then won two playoff contests to get to the Super Bowl in Glendale, Arizona, as 12-point favorites. League MVP Tom Brady had thrown 50 touchdowns, 27 more than Manning. They looked…well…unstoppable.

New York's defense stopped the Pats. The Giants sacked Brady five times, pressured him all night, and kept New England's powerful offense off-balance. And the Giants did just enough with the ball to stay close until the fourth quarter.

Manning guided them on two touchdown drives in the final period. The first ended with David Tyree's 5-yard catch. Then, after the Patriots marched 80 yards to go ahead 14–10, Manning told his teammates in the huddle: "We can do this."

They did, helped by Tyree's "miracle" catch.

Eli Manning holds the Vince Lombardi Trophy next to Head Coach Tom Coughlin after winning his first Super Bowl.

WE WANTED IT MORE

Facing third down and 5 at the New England 44, Manning was trapped and about to be sacked. Not much of a scrambler, he somehow broke free and launched a high pass toward Tyree, who was double covered. Tyree out-jumped the defenders, trapped the ball with one hand against his helmet, and caught it as he fell to the ground.

Moments later, Manning threw the winning 13-yard pass to Plaxico Burress. A few minutes after that, he and the Giants were lifting the Lombardi Trophy as champions of the NFL.

Eli Manning had beaten the unbeatable.

T here always was a challenge for Eli Manning when he was growing up. Having two older brothers who are stars in just about every sport can cause that.

Elisha Nelson Manning is the youngest of the three brothers. By the time Eli was old enough to play organized sports, Cooper

Chapter 2

The Kid Brother

Eli Manning, standing with his brother Peyton, holds up a Giants jersey after being traded during the 2004 NFL Draft. Peyton is perhaps Eli's biggest fan and supporter.

and Peyton were the best players in their New Orleans neighborhood. They always encouraged Eli to follow their leads.

"I played every sport out there. Whatever season it was, that's what we were out playing," Eli said. "Just trying to get better at each of them, that was our philosophy."

"My parents and brothers always made sports fun. I enjoyed being outside and with my friends and having pickup games and just the entertainment of playing sports. It was not so much about the winning and losing to my parents, ever, it was more about making sure we were having a good time."

For Eli, keeping up with his brothers was tough because of their age difference. But learning from them came naturally.

"Cooper and Peyton taught me about enjoying teamwork and building a team together and having a common goal and working together to achieve it," he said. "About making people around you better. And the values you learn in sports."

Those values would come in handy in life, too.

Eli Manning was the quietest of the three brothers, barely saying a word at the dinner table. But he soaked in all the knowledge from his father Archie. A college football great at Ole Miss, Archie also was an NFL quarterback for 14 seasons. Eli also listened intently to his mother, Olivia, and Cooper and Peyton. He was bonding with his siblings without fully understanding why they hung out with him so often.

Eli's father, Archie Manning, was the starting quarterback for the NFL's New Orleans Saints from 1971 to 1981.

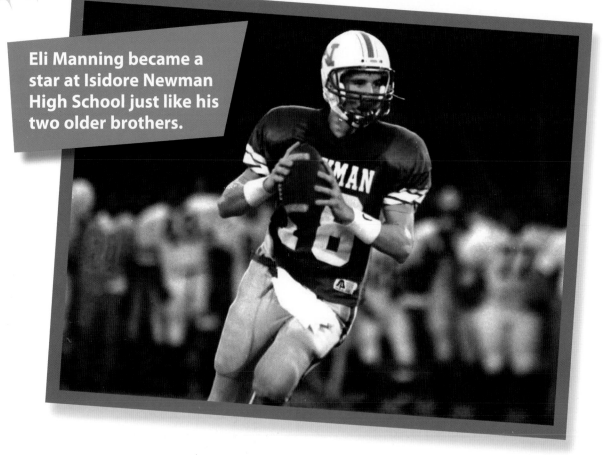

Eli Manning became a star at Isidore Newman High School just like his two older brothers.

"I always thought they enjoyed being around me; they were babysitting me a lot of times," Eli said. "Then I found out they had been grounded and that's why they had to babysit me."

"But they are my heroes, the ones I looked up to when we were growing up. I definitely was copying them, trying to be like them. I enjoyed being the little brother."

By the time he was in the eighth grade, Eli was the only Manning boy living at home. He would go out for dinner with his mom and they would chat about him. Eli was the focus of family talks for the first time. He believed that helped him mature.

When he moved on to high school, Eli really had lots to keep up with. Cooper and Peyton had been stars at Isidore Newman, a private school that was able to beat many larger public schools because of the Manning boys' play. Newman went 34–5 with Peyton at quarterback and he was selected the 1993–94 Gatorade National Football Player of the Year.

Could Eli match that?

Just about. Eli threw for 7,389 yards and 89 touchdowns. That was 200 yards more than Peyton but three fewer scores.

"I'm not trying to cop out," Frank Gendusa, who coached both Peyton and Eli at Newman, told ESPN. com, "but it's impossible to say which one was a better quarterback when I had them."

Following in someone's very successful footsteps is hard, especially when that someone is your father.

One reason Peyton Manning did not attend the University of Mississippi was that his father, Archie, was the greatest quarterback the Rebels ever had. He was a two-time All-

Chapter 3

Following Archie's Footsteps

American, and finished in the top five for the Heisman Trophy. Then he was the No. 2 overall draft pick by the NFL's New Orleans Saints in 1972. Archie even had a song in his honor: "The Ballad of Archie Who."

Although Peyton skipped Ole Miss for Tennessee, younger brother Eli decided to become a Rebel. His oldest brother, Cooper, had gone to Ole Miss, but

Eli was one of the best quarterbacks to ever come from Ole Miss. He is shown here handing the ball off to future New York Giants teammate Brandon Jacobs.

23

he was a receiver. Eli was a star quarterback in high school and he knew he would be compared with his father at Mississippi.

"My parents wanted me to go to the best school for me," Eli said. "They understood that it was a decision I needed to make."

Eli did speak with his older brothers, mainly to get a feel for what it was like to be recruited by dozens of schools. With Texas, Georgia, LSU, Florida, and Tennessee hot on his trail, he chose Mississippi.

Eli knew everything he did at Ole Miss would be matched against what Archie did there, or what Peyton did at Tennessee.

"When he plays against Auburn they're going to say, 'Your father did this against Auburn and your brother did this against Auburn. What are you going to do against Auburn?'" Peyton said.

And those comparisons didn't bother Eli at all. "They remember here," he said. "But it's not something that keeps me up at night."

It turned out to be the right decision, too, because Eli's career at Ole Miss was pretty special.

As a freshman, Eli was a backup and the team was invited to the Music City Bowl against West Virginia. They were behind 49–16 in the final quarter when Head Coach David Cutcliffe put in Eli. He threw for three touchdowns, and the starting job was his.

Some people believe his sophomore season was his best. He guided a so-so team to a 7–4 record while

Ole Miss head coach David Cutcliffe congratulates Eli after a Rebels victory in the 2002 Independence Bowl.

throwing for 31 TDs and setting 17 school records. In a tiring seven-overtime defeat to Arkansas, he threw for six scores.

"There wasn't really a loser," Manning recalled. "We just came up short."

Eli's junior year was disappointing as the Rebels went 6–6. NFL teams were eager for him to turn pro, but he did not want to leave Ole Miss.

So he stayed for his senior season in 2003 and he was sensational. While passing for 3,600 yards and 29 touchdowns, he guided Mississippi to a 10–3 record. Eli won the Maxwell Award as the nation's best all-around player.

Manning had arrived at college with "Eli's Coming" pins and signs on campus. He left with more than 10,000 yards passing, 81 touchdowns, just 35 interceptions and a 24–13 record. The Rebels won two bowl games behind Eli: 27–23 over Nebraska in the 2002 Independence Bowl, and 31–28 over Oklahoma State in the Cotton Bowl in 2004.

The victory over Oklahoma State was Ole Miss' first in a January game since a guy named Archie

Manning led the Rebels past Arkansas in the 1970 Sugar Bowl. It allowed the Rebels to get their first 10-win season since 1971.

"Everything about this year has been great. It's been a great run...it's been a fun ride," Manning said.

He would next be catching a ride to New York— by way of San Diego.

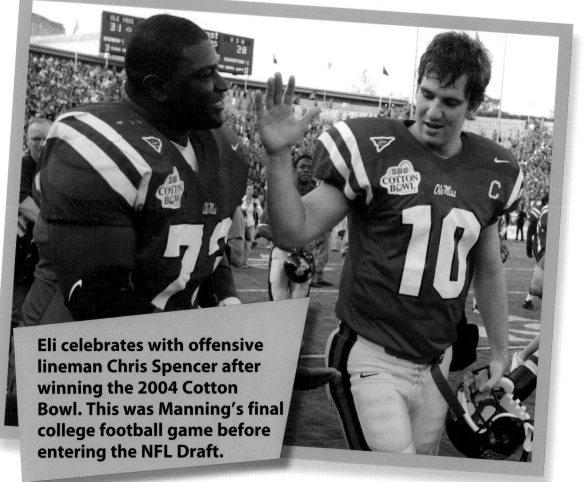

Eli celebrates with offensive lineman Chris Spencer after winning the 2004 Cotton Bowl. This was Manning's final college football game before entering the NFL Draft.

Eli Manning very much wanted to be the first pick in the 2004 NFL Draft, just as older brother Peyton was taken No. 1 overall by Indianapolis six years earlier.

There was one problem. Eli and his father, longtime NFL quarterback and former Ole Miss great Archie Manning, preferred he not be taken by San Diego.

Chapter 4

Heading to the Big Apple

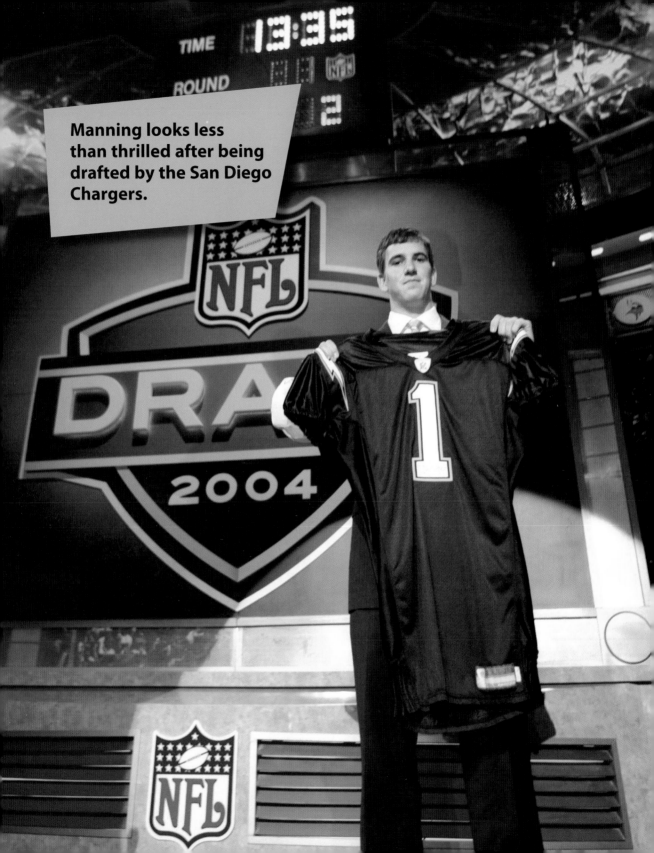

Manning looks less than thrilled after being drafted by the San Diego Chargers.

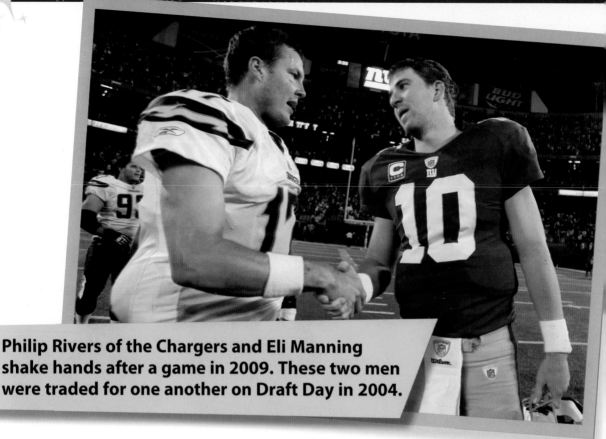

Philip Rivers of the Chargers and Eli Manning shake hands after a game in 2009. These two men were traded for one another on Draft Day in 2004.

The Chargers "earned" the top selection by going 4–12 the previous season. And they needed a quarterback.

But Archie, who had spent most of his career being battered around with a bad New Orleans team, feared the Chargers would be just as awful as those Saints were. He hoped a trade could be worked out to get Eli to an organization the Mannings felt was a better fit for him.

San Diego did not want to hear about it, even after talking with Archie when NFL commissioner Paul Tagliabue arranged a meeting. And when the time came to make their pick opening the draft, the Chargers called out the name Eli Manning.

Up to the stage Eli went, shaking hands with the commissioner and putting on a Chargers cap. He was not smiling.

"The strategy was simple," Chargers coach Marty Schottenheimer said. "Take the player who had the most value. He had the most value in a trade."

But the Mannings did not know that until three picks later. The Giants used up about ten minutes of the fifteen they were allowed before finally swinging a trade with San Diego. New York chose another quarterback, Philip Rivers of North Carolina State. They then dealt him to the Chargers along with a first-round pick the next year.

Welcome to Broadway and the Meadowlands, Eli. And now, Eli was all smiles.

Kurt Warner (left) stands beside Eli Manning during preseason practice in 2004. Manning backed up Warner for the first nine games of his rookie season.

"I feel a lot better than I did ten minutes ago," he said while attending his second news conference at the draft, this one as a New York Giant.

Looking back, Eli admits that was not the most fun day, at least until the trade was announced.

"I didn't want to hurt anyone or insult anyone, but it was important to me to be in a place like this," he said years later.

The Giants had a veteran quarterback in Kerry Collins, but he left for Oakland. Collins was replaced by another veteran, Kurt Warner. A few years earlier, Warner had won a Super Bowl as a member of the St. Louis Rams. Eli began his rookie season on the bench behind Warner. The Giants went 5–4 with Warner at quarterback.

But Head Coach Tom Coughlin knew his future was brightest with Eli. He was right.

By 2005, Eli Manning was the full-time starting quarterback in New York. In just his second season, he led his team into the playoffs.

Although Manning was learning as he played, he helped the Giants go 11–5 to win the NFC East. He threw for 24 touchdowns, but also for 17 interceptions. And even though the Giants scored

Chapter 5

Mr. Clutch

422 points, some fans weren't thrilled with Eli as their QB. New York was shut out 23–0 at home by Carolina in the playoffs. Manning had an awful game, and his critics became louder.

That did not change in 2006 when the Giants opened the schedule by losing to good old Peyton Manning and the Colts. It was a matchup that no one in the family felt comfortable with.

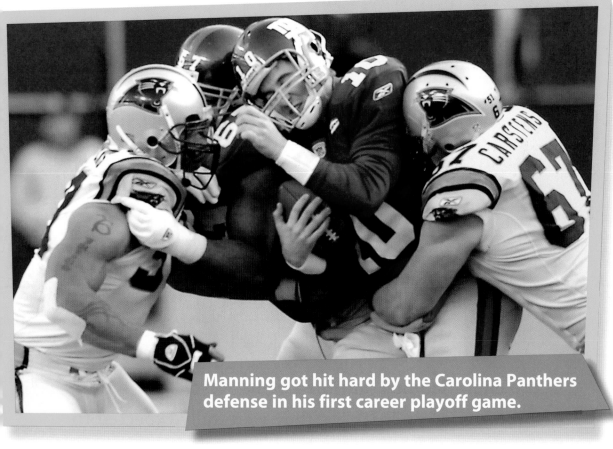

Manning got hit hard by the Carolina Panthers defense in his first career playoff game.

"I'm glad we don't have to go through this for a few more years," said their mom, Olivia Manning. "I guess I'd take it if they managed to get to a Super Bowl together. That would be all right."

There would be no Super Bowl for Eli in 2006 as the Giants slumped to 8–8, losing a wild-card playoff game to Philadelphia. Peyton, however, won his first NFL championship.

The next season the Giants thrilled fans with the magical run of 2007. Manning and New York racked up road wins in the playoffs at Tampa, Dallas, and Green Bay. Eli followed those games up with his MVP performance against New England. It was the second straight Lombardi Trophy to add to the family collection.

As a champion, Manning wanted to show it was no fluke. But it would take another four seasons to prove that. The Giants would be good for a few years, and so would Eli. But they were not great.

The 2011 season, though, was great—at least at the end. Manning and the Giants were coming off a 10–6 record in 2010. So, they were fully expected to chase a championship. Yet they were very streaky in 2011, with two strings of three wins, but also a four-game slide. After losing to a weak Washington team, the Giants were 7–7.

"We know what we have to do, and that's to win every time we play," Manning said. "We put ourselves in a tough spot and we have to fight our way out of it."

There was no question they would play hard. They also played well, very well, led by their quarterback setting three team passing records.

Wins over the Jets and Dallas earned the Giants a playoff

Manning and Head Coach Tom Coughlin are cherishing the Vince Lombardi Trophy after their first Super Bowl victory.

Green Bay was the hottest team going into the 2011 playoffs. Manning threw for three touchdowns against the Packers in a 37–20 victory.

spot, finishing the regular season 9–7. The Giants then beat Atlanta 24–2 at home to open the playoffs. Next, New York was on to frigid Lambeau Field to play the 15–1 Green Bay Packers. Yes, the same place where Manning starred in beating Brett Favre and the Packers four years earlier.

And they did it again! Eli outplayed NFL MVP Aaron Rodgers, passing for three touchdowns in a 37–20 victory.

It was on to the Super Bowl! The Giants would face off against the Patriots again.

Once more, New England was favored. Once more, the Giants ignored the so-called "experts."

"Anytime you go onto the field, you can win," Manning said.

You certainly can when your quarterback completes 30 of 40 pass attempts, including a perfect 38-yarder to Mario Manningham that fell into his hands over two defenders along the sideline. Ahmad Bradshaw's 6-yard run gave the Giants that win, 21–17.

Soon after accepting the trophy at Lucas Oil Stadium in Indianapolis, Giants owner John Mara was asked what stands out about Eli Manning.

"Just that he has something that very few players have," Mara said, "the ability to put a team on his shoulders and carry them."

Carry them all the way to the top.

li Manning holds many charities close to his heart, especially those involving children.

"It's very important to me to be able to give back to the community, and I take a lot of pride in being involved with these causes and charities," he said. "My parents taught me the importance of being able to help and to share."

Chapter 6

Making a Difference

In 2007, Manning began a five-year campaign to raise $2.5 million for the construction of The Eli Manning Children's Clinic. It is in a hospital for children that is part of the University of Mississippi Medical Center. He said he was "humbled by the work they do." Nearly $3 million was raised.

The next year, *USA Weekend* magazine chose Eli as its Most Caring Athlete for his work in the community. He was a member of the President's Council on

Eli is shown here working out with children during an exercise program he helped set up between the NFL and the American Heart Association.

41

Physical Fitness and Sports and has worked with the American Heart Association and with the NFL on PLAY60. That national youth movement promotes physical fitness and healthy living for children.

Eli has taken an active role with the March of Dimes and has partnered with Samsung and its Hope for Children program to improve resources at schools

Eli and his mother, Olivia, work a pancake cooking contest. In return, Sears donated $10,000 to the Eli and Abby Manning Birthing Center.

and hospitals throughout the United States. Thanks to his help working with Samsung, more than $1 million in technology donations have gone to American schools, and then to hospitals, particularly those that care for children.

Eli has joined Peyton as an ambassador of reading for Scholastic's ClassroomsCare, which gets children to read and results in 1 million books being donated.

In 2005, after Hurricane Katrina hit their hometown of New Orleans, Eli and Peyton flew to the area. They helped deliver 30,000 pounds of relief supplies to people who had lost their homes or been injured.

"There are people who are fortunate to be in a position like I am in, and you need to use that position to help others," Eli said. "I am proud to do it."

Career Statistics

Year	Team	Games	Att	Comp	Pct	Yds	TD	Int
2004	Giants	9	197	95	48.2	1,043	6	9
2005	Giants	16	557	294	52.8	3,762	24	17
2006	Giants	16	522	301	57.7	3,244	24	18
2007	Giants	16	529	297	56.1	3,336	23	20
2008	Giants	16	479	289	60.3	3,238	21	10
2009	Giants	16	509	317	62.3	4,021	27	14
2010	Giants	16	539	339	62.9	4,002	31	25
2011	Giants	16	589	359	61.0	4,933	29	16
2012	Giants	16	536	321	59.9	3,948	26	15
	TOTALS	137	4,457	2,612	58.6	31,527	211	144

Att = Attempts   Pct = Completion Percentage   TD = Touchdowns
Comp = Completions   Yds = Yards   Int = Interceptions

Where to Write

ELI MANNING
c/o NEW YORK GIANTS
1925 Giants Drive
East Rutherford, NJ
07073

All-America—One of the best college players in the United States for that year. This is voted on by sportswriters.

American Heart Association—A group whose goal is to promote healthier lifestyles and help people avoid heart diseases.

Big Apple—Nickname for New York City.

bowl—A postseason college football game where teams are invited to compete.

College Football Hall of Fame—Located in South Bend, Indiana, this museum honors the history and greatest players of college football.

Comeback Player of the Year—An award given to a player who has performed well after missing most or all of the previous season.

commissioner—In football, the person hired by the owners of the NFL teams to represent and guide the league.

Heisman Trophy—An award given each year to the best player in college football.

Hurricane Katrina—A devastating storm that struck the Gulf Coast region of the United States and elsewhere in 2005. Over 1,800 people died as a result of the storm.

Lombardi Trophy—Award given to the team that wins the Super Bowl. It was named after former Packers head coach Vince Lombardi, whose teams won the first two Super Bowls.

March of Dimes—A nonprofit group founded by President Franklin Roosevelt, originally to fight polio. In 1958 the group's mission changed to fight birth defects and premature births.

Maxwell Award—Award given each year to the best all around player in college football.

Most Valuable Player (MVP)—Award given to the best player in the league.

National Football Conference (NFC)—The NFL conference in which the New York Giants play.

National Football League (NFL)—A thirty-two team league for pro football.

Ole Miss—The nickname for the University of Mississippi.

pickup game—When a group of people get together to play a sport without referees or officials.

playoffs—A series of games played after the regular season to determine a league champion.

PLAY60—A campaign started by the NFL to encourage kids to be active for sixty minutes per day.

quarterback—The player who takes the snap from the center and either hands off, runs, or throws the ball to other players. Sometimes he's referred to as the "field general" because he is in charge.

sack—When a quarterback is knocked to the ground before he can pass the ball behind the line of scrimmage.

Super Bowl—The championship game of the NFL.

touchdown—When a player gets into the end zone with the ball. It is worth six points.

wild card—The opening round of the NFL playoffs.

wide receiver—The player who stands to the outside when the ball is snapped and usually catches passes.

Read More

Books

Nagle, Jeanne. *Archie, Peyton, and Eli Manning.* Australia: ReadHowYouWant, 2012.

Sandler, Michael. *Eli Manning and the New York Giants: Super Bowl XLVI.* New York: Bearport Publishing, 2012.

Savage. Jeff. *Eli Manning.* Minneapolis, Minn.: Lerner Publications Company, 2012.

Internet Addresses

Official Web Site of the New York Giants
http://www.nfl.com/giants

Eli Manning Statistics
http://www.pro-football-reference.com/players/M/MannEl00.htm

National Football League
http://www.nfl.com

Index